DOUBLED SHADOWS

DOUBLED SHADOWS
重影

Selected poetry of
Ouyang Jianghe
欧阳江河

Translated from Chinese by
Austin Woerner

Zephyr Press & The Chinese University Press of Hong Kong
Brookline, Mass | Hong Kong

Cover image by Xu Bing
Book design by *type*slowly
Printed in Hong Kong

This publication is supported by the Jintian Literary Foundation. Zephyr Press
also acknowledges with gratitude the financial support of The National
Endowment for the Arts and the Massachusetts Cultural Council.

Zephyr Press, a non-profit arts and education 501(c)(3) organization,
publishes literary titles that foster a deeper understanding of cultures
and languages. Zephyr books are distributed to the trade in the U.S.
and Canada by Consortium Book Sales and Distribution [www.cbsd.com]
and by Small Press Distribution [www.spdbooks.org].

Published for the rest of the world by:
The Chinese University Press
The Chinese University of Hong Kong
Sha Tin, N.T., Hong Kong

Cataloguing-in publication data is available from the Library of Congress.

ZEPHYR PRESS
www.zephyrpress.org

JINTIAN
www.jintian.net

THE CHINESE UNIVERSITY PRESS
www.chineseupress.com

CONTENTS

III.

INTRODUCTION
Wolfgang Kubin

Chinese poetry since 1979 has been both a miracle and a disaster. In 1979 China opened her doors to the world, and young poets immediately became a driving force for political reform. The demands they expressed in verse were well understood, and many young people read and wrote poetry that envisioned a new (socialist) society. After thirty years of experiment with free verse and vernacular (白话 *baihua*) poetry (1919–1949) and thirty years of ideological indoctrination that turned literature into a political tool (1949–1979), the "modern poem" (新诗 *xinshi*) sprung into being at the end of the 1970s, mature in both form and in content, its representative products instantly recognizable as an important part of world literature. In and outside of China poets such as Bei Dao 北岛, Gu Cheng 顾城 or Duo Duo 多多 were seen as lyrical voices heralding a new era in contemporary Chinese poetry. They were translated eagerly and discussed worldwide. Though criticized by conservative officials as "obscure" (朦胧 *menglong*), immoral, and politically dubious, these poets made their way into the hearts of Chinese readers. This is the miracle of contemporary Chinese poetry.

And what is the disaster? Moreso than the end of the democracy movement in June 1989, it was the 1992 launch of market reforms, intended to vault China to world-power status, that thrust contemporary Chinese literature into an uncertain new space. Because of the growing complexity of Chinese society, poets who emerged at this time, such as Ouyang Jianghe 欧阳江河, demanded that Chinese literature shed its outdated, black-and-white, simplistically political modes of expression and devote itself entirely to problems of aesthetics and language.

This retreat to literature for its own sake did not mean that the "post-obscure poets" (后朦胧诗派 *hou menglong shipai*) who came to prominence after 1989 were out of touch with the world or truly apolitical. Rather, political issues became a hidden matter, discussed in a complex new language invented to evade censorship. We can see this in the poem "Crossing the Square at Dusk" (傍晚穿过广场 *Bangwan Chuanguo Guangchang*), which deals indirectly with the incidents of Tiananmen and June Fourth. Poems like these could be published on the Mainland only because China's publishers-cum-censors could not keep pace with the increasingly sophisticated language of the poets. At the Qinghai Lake Poetry Festival in August 2011, Ouyang, commenting upon "Crossing the Square," remarked that the events of 1989 are the basis for all recent Chinese poetry. A good poem must reclaim history; it cannot avoid it or digest it. In this way the poet reconstructs history's turning points, enacting them on the lyrical stage. "Crossing the Square" is a prime example of such a poem.

The awakening to the problem of language reflects a vast sea-change in Chinese literature post-1992. Many poets fell silent, and not a few writers gave up literature in favor of making money in the Special Economic Zones. Novelists especially began writing for the market, and poets were relegated to the edges of society. The novel now dominates the literary scene so much that even internationally renowned poets have no more readers at home than abroad—in both cases, very few. Often they must pay to publish their books, or else print their own small editions to distribute for free among friends and scholars in hopes of finding readers and translators. This sudden degradation in the status of poets in China is what I call the disaster of contemporary Chinese poetry.

Confronted with the gradual decline of the Chinese language since 1949, Ouyang, in a dialogue with Chinese and foreign poets some years ago, raised the question: "What is good Chinese?" In his eyes, the Chinese language has turned into a vehicle for propaganda, be it politically since 1949 or economically since 1992. Even the language poets use has degenerated under the impact of Maoist speech (毛体 *maoti*) into "the language of mice" (老鼠的语言 *laoshu de yuyan*). In order to restore the former power of Chinese as found in the parables of the Daoist philosopher Zhuangzi, one must, Ouyang says, strive for "the language of the leopard" (豹的语言 *bao de yuyan*). He gives voice to this sentiment in a poem about the Song Dynasty poet Huang Tingjian 黄庭坚 (1045–1105) which envisions writing as a hunt for the leopard. Through this hunt, the poet is able to restore the lost dignity of both word and object. Poems such as "Handgun" (手枪 *Shouqiang*) and "Glass Factory" (玻璃工厂 *Boli Gongchang*) make the complex relationship between language and reality the subject of discussion. According to Ouyang Jianghe, contemporary speech acts in China render things nonexistent; what is left is only the ideas of things, not the things themselves. Therefore we must make language transparent as glass, disassemble it like a handgun. In this way writing becomes an act of "revenge" (报复 *baofu*).

Besides being endangered by politics and economics, Chinese is also endangered by English, the subject of Ouyang's wry poem "Between Chinese and English" (汉英之间 *Han Ying Zhijian*). As English becomes fashionable, Chinese are increasingly abandoning their own language for a foreign tongue, and even Chinese writers have begun producing literature in English. In most cases the result is the same: the new language is artistically immature, and the mother tongue becomes skewed.

There is a third problem plaguing contemporary Chinese literature: the problem of tradition. Unlike in Western countries, where cultural heritage is often the foundation of literary production, Chinese tradition does not play a prominent role in contemporary Chinese poetry. The reader must be familiar with Western, not Chinese, tradition in order to recognize where Chinese poets come from and the background against which they draft their verses. In most cases it is modern Anglo-American literature that has most influenced poets like Wang Jiaxin 王家新 or Zhai Yongming 翟永明. Thus Yu Jian's 于坚 critique that certain contemporary Chinese poets have ceased to be Chinese poets seems justified at first glance. However, the question is more complicated. What the Kunming-based poet advocates is a poetry more-or-less based on Chinese folk tradition; it is precisely this kind of thinking that, in my opinion, makes the works of China's conservative contemporary poets so drab and uninteresting. I fear the return to "tradition" is an outdated model. All superb poetry is international poetry—it is no longer "national." This is true both for modern American literature under the impact of classical Chinese aesthetics—Ezra Pound is the best example—and for contemporary Chinese literature. Bei Dao comes to mind as such a poet, influenced as he was by the Spanish hermetic poetry of the 1930s. A true "Chinese" writer is a contradiction. Without the inspiration of foreign literature, he or she would just reproduce antiquated forms, adding no new life to the art he or she practices, as can be seen in the works of popular novelists who rehash the storytelling traditions of past dynasties. Only as an international writer can a writer nowadays be a "national" writer. This is the case for Ouyang Jianghe. He writes about both foreign topics ("Picasso Paints a Bull" 毕加索画牛 *Bijiasuo Hua Niu*) and Chinese topics ("Notes Toward a Fiction of the Market Economy" 关于市场经济的虚构笔记 *Guanyu Shichang Jingji de Xugou Biji*). He writes in Chinese, but reflects upon the German poetry of Hölderlin in his dialogues with Zhang Zao 张枣. He lives in Beijing, but often stays in the U.S. (thanks to his green card). He accepts invitations from literary institutions abroad and reads and writes poetry all over the world. He is a frequent visitor to Germany, where in 1997 he did a half-year residency at Castle Solitude near Stuttgart. Unlike the "national" Chinese poets, who rarely go abroad and do not seek dialogue with colleagues from other countries, Ouyang Jianghe is fond of exchanges with German and American writers. It is not only his work but the poet himself who now belongs to world literature.

Has Ouyang Jianghe solved the problems he raised? His own answer to those questions seems to lie in his praxis of writing poems and not in a single refined theory, at least so far. He practices a difficult art of poetry: its complex grammar, its rich and unusual vocabulary, and its new view of the relationship between poet and society demand much from the reader and from any translator. It is not true that the Chinese audience would understand this poetry better than its foreign connoisseur. A reader unfamiliar with the international scene of modern and contemporary poetry will not comprehend a single word, even if he or she is Chinese. And a specialist in world poetry might develop a feeling for what the author is aiming at, even if he or she is not Chinese.

Ouyang was born in 1956 in the province of Sichuan. Along with the poets Zhai Yongming and Zhang Zao, he formed the group now known as the "Five Masters" of Sichuan (五君子 *wu junzi*, lit. "Five Gentlemen"). In the eighties he left Chengdu for Beijing. In the late nineties, after his initial success with the short-form poem, he decided to stop writing, fearing he would write too much and repeat himself. He is a man who struggles hard to live up to his own unforgiving expectations. Now he has taken up the pen again, dedicating himself instead to the long-form poem under the influence of modern French poetry.

Ouyang Jianghe is not only one of the most important poets in the Chinese language today; he is also an influential critic and a renowned calligrapher. Until recent years he made his living introducing Western classical music to the Chinese record industry. Nowadays, he earns his keep with his brush-pen: when not writing essays or book critiques, he devotes himself to the art of the Chinese character. His calligraphy, which is published in book form and sold in galleries, is highly valued and eagerly sought after by collectors. Thus, Ouyang Jianghe does not fit the image of the "poor poet" suffering for his art, desperate to be heard by any who will listen. Rather, he is a member of the new Chinese middle class, living in a modern condominium surrounded by walls and watched over by doormen. There is no free admission to him allowed.

—*Bonn, August 2011*

TRANSLATOR'S FOREWORD
Austin Woerner

It is tempting to imagine that, as a translator working directly with a living author, one might be able to circumvent the written words entirely and delve straight into the author's imagination, digesting the work back into its basic inspirational impulses and reassembling it, alive and breathing, in one's own language. If this were possible—so the myth goes—translation would be no different from the act of creation, and the result would not be a secondary text but another primary one, as faithful to the author's vision as the original. It might even be possible to create a text *more* faithful to it, and one might be justified in whatever radical detours were necessary to reach this end.

Needless to say, this is an extreme sort of thought experiment. No writer can be a fly on the inside of another's skull, and most readers of foreign literature would like a guarantee that they are reading more or less what the foreign reader sees on the page. But any translator who enjoys direct access to their author and the gift of that author's patience in answering endless queries (I was lucky enough to have both) must, to some degree, harbor this fantasy. So I confess that when on a May morning two years ago I first strode through the gate of Ouyang Jianghe's neo-Gothic apartment tower in northeast Beijing, I felt as if I held the key to his intricate, sometimes inscrutable poems. I imagined that, by picking them apart line by line with their creator, I might unlock the mystery that flashes temptingly through the words, and with it animate my own versions.

For almost two weeks we met every day for several hours, dissecting selections from his oeuvre. Sitting at the dining room table in his airy calligraphy-hung flat, sipping green tea out of an Irish coffee glass, I would listen to Ouyang, a slight man with close-cropped hair and the gift of energetic, serious gab, discourse at length about the failure of the Chinese literary tradition to grapple with the physical world, or point out myriad connections between small details in his poems: look, here's an upward motion, here's a downward one; here's light, here's dark; here's white, here's black. Yet when I pressed him too hard about what lay behind the words—what they might hint at, imply, evoke—he would bristle impatiently.

"Listen, you don't have to *get* everything. Just translate the words. Sometimes the reader isn't supposed to know."

Let me step back a moment and explain that for a non-native speaker of a language, even a fluent one, navigating a literary text can feel like being face-blind at a cocktail party. You might understand every element of a sentence, yet somehow its import is lost upon you, like staring hard at a pair of eyes, a nose, and a mouth and failing to recognize your boss or your high-school buddy. Take for example these lines from "Dinner" (晚餐 *Wancan*), translated "literally":

> A hand-carved ivory toothpick stirs slowly
> between loose teeth, in the depths
> of food's eclipse.

What does this mean? What does it tell us about the speaker's psychic state? Is a hand-carved ivory toothpick a luxury item or an heirloom? Are his teeth loose because he is old, or because of a dental condition? And what the hell is "food's eclipse"? The words are there, but their meaning—rather, their poetic argument—is gone.

I found it hard to believe that a Chinese poet with an encyclopedic knowledge of Western poetry, encountered mostly in translation (Pound, Stevens, and St. John Perse are as deep or deeper influences than, say, Du Fu or Huang Tingjian) could seriously believe it was possible to "just translate the words." So one day I came prepared to win him over with what I thought was a killer analogy.

"Imagine," I said, readying pen and paper, "that you want me to make a painting. You tell me the painting is of a forest, and peeking from behind one of the trees is a tail. I ask you what kind of animal is hiding behind the trees. You say you don't want to tell me, because you don't want me to paint the whole animal.

"But if I paint a tail, I can't *not* make a decision about what kind of animal it might be. It might look like this . . .

 or this . . . or this."

"Ah-hah!" Ouyang said, grabbing the pen. "That's where you're wrong. *This* is the tail I want you to paint."

This seemed to end the debate.

The "Tail in the Forest" analogy became a touchstone for me and Ouyang. It is, perhaps, the foundation upon which my technique for translating him is built. To use a metaphor Ouyang is fond of, language is like glass. A more concrete, traditional poem—one with a single implied narrative, or scene—is like a lens through which the reader sees a *thing*. The translator's job is to create a new lens through which readers in his language can see the same thing. But Ouyang's poetry—like the best "abstract" or "difficult" modern Western poetry (from Crane and Stevens to Palmer and Armantrout), and like some of the most powerful traditional Chinese poetry—functions more like a prism or kaleidoscope. It bends, refracts, and sometimes scatters the light of meaning; through it the reader perceives not one thing but numerous shifting images cast by their own imagination. *What* the reader sees is less important than the *manner* in which the prism bends the light. My role is to replicate the shape of the prism. In other words, it's to just translate the words.

But to just translate the words—to leave the animal behind the trees as undefined as possible—is trickier than it sounds. Translating from Chinese to English forces the translator to make all kinds of decisions the Chinese writer can leave ambiguous. Minute decisions about articles, verb tense, or word order can turn what should be a profound utterance into an utterly plebeian one. Take, for example, two possible versions of the opening of Ouyang's seminal poem "Glass Factory" (玻璃工厂 *Boli Gongchang*):

> From seeing to seeing: between is only glass.
> Between face and face
> the separation cannot be seen.
> But in glass, matter is not transparent.
> [...]

> The thing between seeing and seeing is glass.
> The separation not seen
> between face and face.
> But glass, as a thing, is not transparent.
> [...]

The version on the bottom gives the mind pause, opens room for imagination; the one on the top merely states the obvious. It is this kind of resonance that is most in danger of being lost when poetry like Ouyang's is translated, and which I must labor to preserve—or recreate.

★

The "Tail in the Forest" incident made me realize I'd been chasing imaginary animals. Whatever was essential about Ouyang's poetry—its spark, its animating principle—did not lie in its meaning. Rather, it had to be something inherent in the very fabric of the words themselves, in the weave of the curtain, the shape of the prism.

As it turns out, the answer had been staring me in the face. It was in the small details Ouyang had pointed out from the beginning—how certain motifs repeated, or were echoed by their opposites; how a vertical motion might follow a horizontal one, light follow dark, black follow white. It was also in the two massive speakers that stood in Ouyang's living room ("listening room" is more accurate) and the roughly 30,000 classical music CDs that lined the walls, their spines arranged in a crenellated fashion for optimum acoustics. Among the Beijing intelligentsia Ouyang is famous as a classical music fanatic, and when our talk flagged we would retire to the "listening room" to, say, compare two performances of the Shostakovich viola sonata, the sounds so precise that every scratch of bow on string or thump of articulated piano key hung palpably in the air.

My first impulse had been to look for the answer to my question in the intangibles of voice and sound—the qualities we are most used to thinking of as poetry's essence, and which are most easily lost upon a foreign reader. But it soon became clear that the sonic qualities of language were not Ouyang's chief concern (though certain poems, like "Sounds of Spring" [春之声 *Chun zhi Sheng*] arise from a kind of word-sound synesthesia). Instead, his poems are rooted in a deeper kind of musicality. He arranges ideas as a composer arranges musical motifs, by repeating them, inverting them, juxtaposing them; over the course of a poem the images chime in an intricate, stylized choreography.

Though this finely-textured, composed quality is present in almost all of Ouyang's poems, it is most salient in his longer pieces, where the interplay of motifs has time to gain momentum. He explained his poem "Our Hunger, Our Sleep" (我们的睡眠，我们的饥饿 *Women de Shuimian, Women de Ji'e*) to me as a string quartet, with four main characters—bat, rat, man, leopard—in the roles of violins, viola, and cello. In each stanza one or more of these characters appears in solo or duet; from stanza to stanza they enter and exit, relationships constantly shifting. The poem unfolds like a fugue, a kind of compositional wind-up toy that, cranked and let run, whirs along on its own potential energy, exhausting all possible permutations until it comes to a halt.

Ouyang treats language as a composer treats sound, as an abstract medium. To him words are bare germs around which meaning may accrue; by manipulating and developing them he builds up a coherent system out of which meaning emerges. His poems are like music in the way that, for Stravinsky, music is like architecture: they serve primarily to create large cathedral-like spaces for the reader to walk around in. To us the leap of an arch may suggest transcendence, but the builder's main concern was that it hold up the roof. Of course, few answer the call of poetry without some predilection for the architectural qualities of language, but Ouyang seems to have done so in the extreme.

*

Replicating the architecture of Ouyang's cathedrals in English can be quite tricky, given that wordplay and double meaning are an inherent part of the masonry. In particular, Ouyang is fond of a type of wordplay possible only in Chinese, whose words are often built out of two paired morphemes, a morphological strategy English uses more sparingly, in compounds like *fishtank, eyeglass, wordplay. Rishi* 日食 (eclipse) means literally *sun-eat*, with *sun* bearing connotations of time, so in "Dinner," a poem about food and time, its appearance feels inevitable. In English, the word vibrates on neither of these frequencies, and some tricky tacking is required to make the image make sense. In other cases, it's simply a matter of choosing one meaning and abandoning the other, as with *kaihe* (opening and closing, as of a door) in "Mother, Kitchen" (母亲，厨房 *Muqin, Chufang*)—to chime with the other images in the poem, it can only be translated as "opening." But sometimes, there is simply no way to do what he is doing. In those cases, I have to get my bearings in English, survey the linguistic landscape, and ask myself: what would Ouyang do here?

When Ouyang and I were in residency at the Vermont Studio Center in 2009, I had a rare chance to watch the architect at work. Ouyang, who had originally planned to write a piece of art criticism, heard the Muse (the philosopher Zhuangzi, actually) calling out of the early-fall air of northern Vermont, and over the next two weeks spun out a new long-form poem, one of the first after his decade-long sabbatical from writing poetry. I had the rare privilege of watching this process unfold, bit by bit, on his laptop screen—from time to time he would summon me with an eager rap on my studio door—and I decided to attempt a simultaneous literary translation.

By observing, and sometimes participating in, Ouyang's creative process, I came as close as I could to being a fly on the inside wall of his mind. Ouyang is a ruthless reviser: his process, he is fond of saying, begins at the point when another writer might call the poem finished. Over the course of the two weeks I watched a single poem divide meiotically into two, then watched one half grow into the poem included in this anthology. When it was nearing maturity he began sending me drafts, each one with the assurance that this, for real, was the final one. I would go to work on it, then the next day, without fail, a new draft would appear in my inbox, and I would have to scrap (or at least deeply reconsider) what I had already done. This continued up till thirty minutes short of the poem's first public reading.

What I saw, as I tussled with each successive version, was that for one thing to change required many other things to change, often in distant parts of the poem. It was as if these bits were quantum-entangled, connected by some invisible thread; this action-at-a-distance proved their relationship, and sometimes illuminated its nature. When a line in stanza 4 changed to *hear . . . the wind-blown snow of a butterfly's dream*, a line in stanza 5 changed too: *Blow lightly, light as wings turned to dust*. The specific thing being echoed was the idea of lightness, the granularity of the snow in the first line and the dust in the second. Snow turns to dust. At the same time, an avalanche in stanza 3 mysteriously disappeared, making room for the line *a banker at the ATM machine inside his own head / presses the button to empty his heart*, and in stanza 2 "paper voices" became "empty voices" (I should note that just to describe these relationships clearly in English I have had to alter the images slightly).

The goal of all this, I came to realize, was not to heighten the poem's intricacy but to simplify it, unify it, and by doing so open up space within it. Like Picasso in "Picasso Paints a Bull," (毕加索画牛 *Bijiasuo Hua Niu*) Ouyang works by subtracting, cutting ruthlessly till most of what he wrote lies in scraps on the floor, and what remains is emptiness, a vessel. And that is the moment—to quote Ouyang—when the poem becomes alive, when it can assimilate anything, and from it things can grow: a tree, human flesh, time.

⋆

So in a sense, my fantasy was fulfilled—I got, if not a glimpse into Ouyang's mind, at least a working sense of how he crafts a poem, what elements drive it, and what is just smoke. When the words proved impossible to translate (which they often did), I could try to translate his vision, which in this case is synonymous with his technique.

My goal has been twofold: first, to replicate the architecture of his poems, the sidestepping flow of images and complex polyphony upon which they're built; and second, to widen the space within—raise the poems' ceilings, suggest hallways leading away. When possible, I tried to use the words Ouyang used; when not possible, I tried to use words or progressions of words he *might* use if writing in English, offered its resources and faced by its limitations. In the opening lines of "Glass Factory," the transformation of "matter" into "thing" might strike Chinese readers as a betrayal; but given that Chinese lacks a single word for "thing," instead subdividing the idea into words like "affair" (事情 *shiqing*), "stuff" (东西 *dongxi*), "object" (事物 *shiwu*), "matter" (物质 *wuzhi*), and given the poem's larger philosophical argument, I find it hard to believe that Ouyang, had English been his native language, would have written such a poem without reaching for the word "thing."

In my own process, I have taken inspiration from Ouyang's Picasso. In my first drafts, in trying to capture not what Ouyang said but how he said it, I inevitably put more of *me* into the poem than many poets and translators would be comfortable with. In subsequent rewritings, I tried to carve away as much of me as possible, leaving mostly Ouyang, without knocking down pillars that hold up the roof. To those alert bilingual readers who plan to compare Chinese and English line by line: you will sometimes find small pieces of Ouyang missing, or bits of me still lodged in the masonry. But the poem, Ouyang might say, is not in the words themselves. It's in the space they create.

DOUBLED SHADOWS
重影

I

玻璃工厂

从看见到看见，中间只有玻璃。
从脸到脸
隔开是看不见的。
在玻璃中，物质并不透明。
整个玻璃工厂是一只巨大的眼珠，
劳动是其中最黑的部分，
它的白天在事物的核心闪耀。
事物坚持了最初的泪水，
就像鸟在一片纯光中坚持了阴影。
以黑暗方式收回光芒，然后奉献。
在到处都是玻璃的地方，
玻璃已经不是它自己，而是
一种精神。
就像到处都是空气，空气近乎不存在。

工厂附近是大海。
对水的认识就是对玻璃的认识。
凝固，寒冷，易碎，
这些都是透明的代价。
透明是一种神秘的、能看见波浪的语言，
我在说出它的时候已经脱离了它，
脱离了杯子、茶几、穿衣镜，所有这些
具体的、成批生产的物质。
但我又置身于物质的包围之中，生命被欲望充满。

Glass Factory

1

The thing between seeing and seeing is glass.
The separation not seen
between face and face.
But glass, as a thing, is not transparent.
A glass factory is a massive eyeball,
labor at its center, whose darkness is daylight
glinting at the cores of things.
A thing persists in its initial tear.
As a bird in pure light persists in its shadow.
Gathers light into darkness, offers it back.
Where glass is everywhere, glass is not itself
but spirit.
As air seems not to exist, where all is air.

2

The glass factory is not far from the sea.
To know water is to know glass.
Cold, solid, fragile: this is the price
at which a thing attains transparence.
Transparence, strange language of seeing waves:
by speaking it I have already left it.
Left behind wineglasses, pictures in frames, the changing-room mirror, all these
specific, mass-produced things.
But I live in things, enveloped by things, a life brimming with want.

语言溢出，枯竭，在透明之前。
语言就是飞翔，就是
以空旷对空旷，以闪电对闪电。
如此多的天空在飞鸟的身体之外，
而一只孤鸟的影子
可以是光在海上的轻轻的擦痕。
有什么东西从玻璃上划过，比影子更轻，
比切口更深，比刀锋更难逾越。
裂缝是看不见的。

3

我来了，我看见，我说出。
语言和时间浑浊，泥沙俱下，
一片盲目从中心散开。
同样的经验也发生在玻璃内部。
火焰的呼吸，火焰的心脏。
所谓玻璃就是水在火焰里改变态度，
就是两种精神相遇，
两次毁灭进入同一永生。
水经过火焰变成玻璃，
变成零度以下的冷漠的燃烧，
像一个真理或一种感情
浅显，清晰，拒绝流动。
在果实里，在大海深处，水从不流动。

Language is overflow, evaporation.
And finally, transparence.
Language is flying: void to void, lightning to lightning. So much sky
outside the body of a flying bird,
and its shadow: a nick of light on the surface of the sea.
A thing cannot leave a mark on glass unless
it is lighter than shadow, deeper than a cut, sheerer than a blade.
A crack cannot be seen.

3

I come, I see, I speak.
Language is clouded with time,
the glimmer sinks with the sediment,
a haze of blindness disperses from the center.
This is the process that occurs within glass.
Flame's heart, flame's breath.
In flame, water experiences a change of perspective.
Two spirits meet, two obliterations become one
eternity.
Water passes through flame and is glass:
a subzero burning, like reason or feeling,
shallow, lucid, rejecting flow.
In fruit, in the depths of the sea, water never flows.

4

那么这就是我看到的玻璃——
依旧是石头，但已不再坚固。
依旧是火焰，但已不复温暖。
依旧是水，但既不柔软也不流逝。
它是一些伤口但从不流血。
它是一种声音但从不经过寂静。
从失去到失去，这就是玻璃。
语言和时间透明，
付出高代价。

5

在同一工厂我看见三种玻璃：
物态的，装饰的，象征的。
人们告诉我玻璃的父亲是一些混乱的石头。
在石头的空虚里，死亡并非终结，
而是一种可改变的原始的事实。
石头粉碎，玻璃诞生。
这是真实的。但还有另一种真实
把我引入另一种境界：从高处到高处。
在那种真实里玻璃仅仅是水，是已经
或正在变硬的、有骨头的、泼不掉的水，
而火焰是彻骨的寒冷，
并且最美丽的也最容易破碎。
世间一切崇高的事物，以及
事物的眼泪。

4

So, this the glass is I see—
still stone, but never strong again,
still flame, but never hot again,
still water, but never gentle, never flowing.
A wound that does not bleed.
A sound that does not pass through silence.
Glass is the thing between loss and loss,
permitting light
like language and time
at a towering price.

5

In one factory I see three kinds of glass.
Substance, ornament, symbol.
They tell me glass is the child of muddled stone.
In the void that is stone, death is not ending
but original, mutable fact.
Stone crumbles, glass is born.
This is real.
But there is another reality that lifts me from this height
to another height, where glass is nothing
but water, a fluid made boned and unflowable,
where flame is a bonechilling cold,
where for a thing to be beautiful it must also be fragile.
All lofty things of this earth
and their tears.

手枪

手枪可以拆开
拆作两件不相关的东西
一件是手，一件是枪
枪变长可以成为一个党
手涂黑可以成为另一个党

而东西本身可以再拆
直到成为相反的向度
世界在无穷的拆字法中分离

人用一只眼睛寻求爱情
另一只眼睛压进枪膛
子弹眉来眼去
鼻子对准敌人的客厅
政治向左倾斜
一个人朝东方开枪
另一个人在西方倒下

黑手党戴上白手套
长枪党改用短枪
永远的维纳斯站在石头里
她的手拒绝了人类
从她的胸脯拉出两只抽屉
里面有两粒子弹，一枝枪
要扣响时成为玩具
谋杀，一次哑火

Handgun (I)

after Ouyang Jianghe

you can take a-
part a handgun, break it
in two, into
a hand   a gun

paint the hand black, you've got
a faction—
put the gun on a boat: that's
a means of persuasion

you can take apart a faction
into further partitions
parties
ambitions
you can break it into act, or action—
the world divides in infinite fissions

one eye you aim
at love; the other you ram
into the barrel of a gun
the bullets ogle
you level your nose at your enemies'
parlors: persuasion
becomes sinidextrous.
you take your hand-
gun, shoot into the west—
in the east, a man falls

the Black Hand puts on white gloves
gunboats volley in private rooms
in stone, eternal Venus stands
her hands rejecting humanity
from her breasts she pulls
a pair of drawers—
two bullets   a gun

pull the trigger: it becomes a toy
murder
hang fire

墨水瓶

纸脸起伏的遥远冬天,
狂风掀动纸的屋顶,
露出笔尖上吸满墨水的脑袋。

如果钢笔拧紧了笔盖,
就只好用削过的铅笔书写。
一个长腿蚊的冬天以风的姿势快速移动。
我看见落到雪地上的深深黑夜,
以及墨水和橡皮之间的
一张白纸。

已经拧紧的笔盖,谁把它拧开了?
已经用铅笔写过一遍的日子,
谁用吸墨水的笔重新写了一遍?

覆盖,永无休止的覆盖。
我一生中的散步被车站和机场覆盖。
擦肩而过的美丽面孔被几个固定的词
            覆盖。
大地上真实而遥远的冬天
被人造的220伏的冬天覆盖。
绿色的田野被灰蒙蒙的一片屋顶覆盖。

而当我孤独的书房落到纸上,
被墨水一样滴落下来的集体宿舍覆盖,
谁是那倾斜的墨水瓶?

Ink Bottle

Paper faces rolling in distant winter:
wind lifts paper rooftops, revealing
the ink-filled mind at the tip of a pen.

If the cap is screwed tight,
no choice but to write with a sharpened pencil.
A spidered winter blows past in the posture of wind.
I see night fallen on snow,
I see, between ink and eraser,
a white page.

Who unscrewed the cap?
Who wrote over my penciled life
with indelible ink?

Covered, forever covered.
A life of footsteps
covered by airports and train stations, a beautiful face
covered by a pat phrase,
the earth's actual, distant winter
covered by a man-made, 220-volt winter.
Green fields covered by sullen rooftops.

When my little studio, fallen to the page,
is covered by the blots of collective dormitories,
who will be the tilted ink bottle?

春之声

从灰暗的外套翻出红色毛衣领子，
高高地挽起裤脚，赤足淌过小河，
喉咙感到融雪的强烈刺痛，
春天的咕咕水泡冒出大地。

早晨翻过身来，阳光灼烧的脊背
像一面斜坡朝午后的低洼处泛起。
春天的有力爪子抓住了
蜷伏在人体里的慵懒黑猫。

梦中到来的大海，我紧紧压住的胸口
在经历了冬眠和干旱之后，又将经历
爱情的滚滚洪水和一束玫瑰。
我的头上野蜂飞舞。

从前是这样：当我动身去远方，
春天的闷罐车已经没有座位。
春天的黑色汽笛涌上指尖，
我放下了捂住耳朵的双手。

现在依旧是这样：春天的四轮马车
在天空中奔驰，我步行回到故乡。
春天的热线电话响成一片。
要是听不到老虎，就只好去听蟋蟀。

Sounds of Spring

From under glum overcoats bright hems peek,
pants are hiked, a river forded barefoot,
the sting of melting snow is felt high in the throat
and the earth offers up the rushing froth of spring.

Morning, rolling over, shows a sunburnt flank
whose slope trickles to the pools of afternoon.
Spring's bright talons tear open the body
and seize the black cat curled within.

Dream of an ocean thundering in: I clutch at my chest
which after hibernation and drought will now weather
love's rollicking tides, and a single bouquet.
Bumblebees murmur at my temples.

How it used to be: standing with bags packed
and not one seat left in the boxcars of spring.
The long black whistle fading to my fingertips
while my hands fall slowly from my ears.

And still spring's carriages course through the sky
while I plod down the road to my hometown.
The shrilling of telephones fills the air.
If I can't hear the tiger, I'll listen to the crickets.

空中小站

下午，我在途中。
远方的小火车站像狼眼睛一样闪耀。

火车站并不远，天黑前能够到达。
我要去的地方是没有黑夜的城市。
警察局长的办公桌放在空无一人的
广场中央，大街上的行人是雕塑，
密探的面孔像雨水在速写的墨水中
变成深色。汽笛响过后
无人乘坐的火车
开出车站，我错过了开车的时间。

有一座上层建筑，顶端是花园。
有一个空中小站，悬于花园之上。
有一段楼梯，高出我的视野。
有一次旅行，通向我对面的座位。
而我从未去过的城市，狂欢的
露天晚宴持续到天明，吹了一夜的风
突然停止，邮件和人事档案漫天飘落。

下午，我在途中。
远方有一个
高于广场和上层建筑的空中小站。

Station in the Air

In the afternoon of my journey
I see, in the distance
lights of a station glittering like wolf's eyes.

A town: we should arrive before nightfall.
In the city where I'm going, there is no night.
An officer's desk commands an empty square,
the people are statues in the streets,
faces of spies darken like rainwater
in hurried brush-strokes. The whistle sounds.
The train, empty, pulls out of the station:
I missed my departure time.

Atop the superstructure there is a garden.
Above the garden there is a station in the air.
A flight of stairs leads up out of my vision.
A journey ends in the seat across from me.
And in a city I've never been to, a wild open-air banquet
rages till dawn, a wind that has blown all night
ceases, and letters and dossiers rain from the sky.

In the afternoon of my journey, I see a station
high above the superstructure, high above the square.

汉英之间

我居住在汉字的块垒里，
在这些和那些形象的顾盼之间。
它们孤立而贯穿，肢体摇晃不定，
节奏单一如连续的枪。
一片响声之后，汉字变得简单。
掉下了一些胳膊，腿，眼睛。
但语言依然在行走，伸出，以及看见。
那样一种神秘养育了饥饿。
并且，省下很多好吃的日子，
让我和同一种族的人分食，挑剔。
在本地口音中，在团结如一个晶体的方言
在古代和现代汉语的混为一谈中，
我的嘴唇像是圆形废墟，
牙齿陷入空旷
没碰到一根骨头。
如此风景，如此肉，汉语盛宴天下。
我吃完我那份日子，又吃古人的，直到

一天傍晚，我去英语角散步，看见
一群中国人围住一个美国佬，我猜他们
想迁居到英语里面。但英语在中国没有领地。
它只是一门课，一种会话方式，电视节目，
大学的一个系，考试和纸。
在纸上我感到中国人和铅笔的酷似。
轻描淡写，磨损橡皮的一生。
经历了太多的墨水，眼镜，打字机
以及铅的沉重之后，
英语已经轻松自如，卷起在中国的一角。
它使我们习惯了缩写和外交辞令，

Between Chinese and English

I live between the bricks of Chinese characters,
in glances exchanged between image and image.
They're separate but continuous, with shifting limbs
and a rhythm uniform as gunfire.
The dust settles: Chinese is simplified.
Off tumble legs, arms, eyes.
But my language still runs, still reaches, sees.
These mysteries give birth to hunger.
And there are plenty of suns and moons left
to linger over with my comrades-in-tongue.
In this vast crystal aggregate of accents and dialects,
this murky admixture of ancient and new,
my mouth is a circular ruin,
teeth plunging into space,
never hitting bone.
Such vistas, such meat: Chinese is a banquet for all.
I eat up my suns and moons, and the ancients' too, till

one evening I walk through the English corner, and see
a bunch of Chinese mobbing an American kid: it seems
they want to make their homes in English.
But in China, English has no sovereign turf.
It's a class, a test, a TV show,
a way of speaking, words on paper.
On paper, we behold our penciled nature.
A sketch, a life of worn erasers.
After centuries of inkwells, spectacles, typewriters,
after years of accumulated lead,
how could English be so light, folded and tucked in our corner?
Now we speak diplospeak, acronyms,

还有西餐，刀叉，阿司匹林。
这样的变化不涉及鼻子
和皮肤，像每天早晨的牙刷
英语在牙齿上走着，使汉语变白。
从前吃书吃死人，因此

我天天刷牙，这关系到水，卫生和比较。
由此产生了口感，滋味说
以及日常用语的种种差异。
还关系到一只手，它伸进英语
中指和食指分开，模拟
一个字母，一次胜利，一种
对自我的纳粹式体验。
一支烟落地，只燃到一半就熄灭了
像一段历史。历史就是苦于口吃的
战争，再往前是第三帝国，是希特勒。
我不知道这个狂人是否枪杀过英语，枪杀过
莎士比亚和济慈。
但我知道，有牛津辞典里的、贵族的英语，
也有武装到牙齿的、邱吉尔或罗斯福的英语。
它的隐喻，它的物质，它的破坏的美学
在广岛和长崎爆炸。
我看见一堆堆汉字在日语中变成尸首——
但在语言之外，中国和英美结盟。
我读过这段历史，感到极为可疑。
我不知道历史和我谁更荒谬。

一百多年了，汉英之间，究竟发生了什么？
为什么如此多的中国人移居英语，
努力成为黄种白人，而把汉语
看作离婚的前妻，看作破镜里的家园？究竟

muffins, aspirin, forks and knives.
But these changes do not affect the nose, the skin:
like the toothbrush you pick up in the morning, English
glides lightly over the teeth, whitening language.
With so much ink caked in my gums, I'd better

brush every day: this requires water, a cleaning agent, and perspective.
It gives rise to theories of taste, and countless
disparities in everyday usage.
It also requires a hand, reaching into English,
two fingers apart, a letter, a triumph,
a Nazi experiment upon the self.
A cigarette falls to the ground still burning
like history, which after all
is what happens when one nation eats another's words.
One step forward, you've got the Third Reich, Hitler.
I don't know if that madman gunned down English,
massacred Shakespeare and Keats.
But I do know that English comes in two flavors:
the noble, alphabetized English of Oxford,
and the English of Churchill and Roosevelt, armed to the teeth.
Its metaphors, its science, its obliterating aesthetics
landed on Hiroshima and Nagasaki.
I watched Chinese characters become Japanese corpses—
but outside of language, our nations are allies.
I've read this history, and I'm suspicious.
I don't know which is crazier, history or me.

What's happened, this past hundred years, between Chinese and English?
Why are so many Chinese streaming into English,
trying hard as they can to blanche their own skin?
Why do they treat their language like an estranged wife,
a home in a broken mirror?

发生了什么？我独自一人在汉语中幽居
与众多纸人对话，空想着英语。
并看着更多的中国人跻身其间
从一个象形的人变为一个拼音的人。

I live alone amid my stacked bricks, conversing
with paper dolls, dreaming in English, while all around me
Chinese mount the steps to English, turning
from people of pictures to people of sound.

Note:

*"English corner" refers to a phenomenon in 1980s China in which a public space,
such as a corner of a city park, would become a gathering-point for students to
practice speaking English.*

交谈

在寂静的客厅里我们交谈了一小时，
空旷、清澈。总是在这样的时刻，
我回头去看一张美丽的面孔
一闪就不见了。一小时的冬天反映在落日里。
我辞别主人时天色已经变暗，
屋里亮着灯，街上的灯也都一起亮了。

看见一张美丽的面孔既幸福又伤心。
在她之前的一切面孔是多么迷惘和短暂。
一小时的注视，这就够了：
客厅通向厨房，冰凉的小手
通向旧日子的一顿晚餐，
远在我伸手去碰纯银的餐具之前。

一小时的交谈，散发出银质的寒冷。
美丽的面孔一闪就不见了。
总是在这样的时刻我回头去看——
客厅里灯光明亮，然而深掩的面孔
不是光芒所能照耀的。深处的交谈
无声无息。一小时的交谈——
十年前，我们是否会谈上一夜？

Conversation

In the quiet of your living room we talked for an hour.
Wide vistas, transparence. Always
at times like these, I look back, see—
a beautiful face flashes
and is gone. An hour of winter
reflected in sunset. We say our goodbyes.
Outside, it's getting dark. Lights
are on in your house, and in all the other houses.

To have seen that face: such pain,
such joy. So many faces before, each
its own kind of incoherent and brief.
An hour is enough: living room
leads to kitchen, to a small cold hand
laying out plates for a meal years before
I reached out my hand to touch
your silver tableware.

Hour of silver, hour of chill.
Face flashes and is gone.
Always at times like these I look back—
The room is bright. A beautiful face
is not a thing that light can reveal.
Deep-hidden face, soundless conversation
in shadow. A single hour—
ten years ago, would we have talked all night?

像忍住泪水那样忍住一小时的柔情怜意。
我的余生不会比这一小时更久长。
消逝是幸福的：美丽的面孔
一闪就不见了。总是在这样的时刻
天色开始变暗。女儿嘟着嘴，
有人在轻轻地敲门。

An hour's tenderness, held back like tears.
The years I have left will speed faster
than this hour. To vanish
is happiness: Flash, face. Be gone.
Always at times like these,
darkness falls. A child pouts,
and someone taps at the door.

星期日的钥匙

钥匙在星期日早上的阳光中晃动。
深夜归来的人回不了自己的家。
钥匙进入锁孔的声音，不像敲门声
那么遥远，梦中的地址更为可靠。

当我横穿郊外公路，所有车灯
突然熄灭。在我头上的无限星空里
有人捏住了自行车的刹把。倾斜，
一秒钟的倾斜，我听到钥匙掉在地上。

许多年前的一串钥匙在阳光中晃动。
我拾起了它，但不知它后面的手
隐匿在何处？星期六之前的所有日子
都上了锁，我不知道该打开哪一把。

现在是星期日。所有房间
全部神秘地敞开。我扔掉钥匙。
走进任何一间房屋都用不着敲门。
世界如此拥挤，屋里却空无一人。

Key to Sunday

A key glints in the Sunday morning light.
A returning traveler is locked out in the dark.
A knock on the door is always more faint
than the rasp of metal in the keyhole.
Only a dreamed address is reliable.

As I bike down a quiet street
all the headlights go out at once.
In the night sky above, a hand clenches a brake.
I hear a clink. A key has fallen to the ground.

I see a ring of keys, keys of years past
glinting in the light. I pick them up.
But where are the hands that hide behind them?
A row of closed days, ending in Saturday—
but I do not know which to unlock.

Now it is Sunday. All the doors on the street
stand open. I toss the keys away.
No need to knock. Just walk right in.
Such a crowded world, and no one at home.

晚餐

香料接触风吹
之后，进入火焰的熟食并没有
进入生铁。锅底沉积多年的白雪
从指尖上升到头颅，晚餐
一直持续到我的垂暮之年。
　　　　　　　　　　不会
再有早晨了。在昨夜，在点蜡烛的
街头餐馆，我要了双份的
卷心菜，空心菜，生鱼片和香肠，
摇晃的啤酒泡沫悬挂。
　　　清帐之后，
一根用手工磨成的象牙牙签
在疏松的齿间，在食物的日蚀深处
慢慢搅动。不会再有早晨了。
晚间新闻在深夜又重播了一遍。
其中有一则讣告：死者是第二次
　　　　　　　　　　　死去。

短暂地注视，温柔地诉说，
为了那些长久以来一直在倾听
和注视我的人。我已替亡灵付帐。
不会再有早晨了，也不会
　　　再有夜晚。

Dinner

After the spice and wind meet, I wait
for a meal that has entered flame
to enter metal. The pot is full
of years accumulated like snow, falling
upward now, from my fingertips to my temples.
I will be eating this dinner till I am bent with age.
                                    There will not be
another morning. Last night, at a roadside
hotpot joint, by the light of a candle, I ordered
dinner for two. Lettuce hearts,
fish, thin nestled slices. In two
glasses of beer, flights of bubbles
rising.
                    I waited for the check
while a toothpick whittled from an elephant's tooth
retraced its course through a constellation
of aches, minor eclipses
of sustenance. There will not be another morning.
On the guttering TV screen, the evening
news repeated its single headline:
                                    the deceased have died
another death.
A glance, a couple words.
For those who all these years have watched
and listened. I see
what it comes to, and I pay.
There will not be another morning, or
                              another night.

傍晚穿过广场

我不知道一个过去年代的广场
从何而始，从何而终。
有的人用一小时穿过广场，
有的人用一生——
早晨是孩子，傍晚已是垂暮之人。
我不知道还要在夕光中走出多远才能
停住脚步？

还要在夕光中眺望多久
才能闭上眼睛？当高速行驶的汽车
打开刺目的车灯。
那些曾在一个明媚早晨穿过广场的人
我从汽车的后视镜看见过他们一闪即逝
的面孔。
傍晚他们乘车离去。

一个无人离去的地方不是广场，
一个无人倒下的地方也不是。
离去的重新归来，倒下的却永远倒下了。
一种叫做石头的东西
迅速地堆积，屹立，
不像骨头的生长需要一百年的时间，
也不像骨头那么软弱。

每个广场都有一个用石头垒起来的脑袋，
使两手空空的人们感到生存的
份量。以巨大的石头脑袋去思考和仰望，
对任何人都不是一件轻松的事。

Crossing the Square at Dusk

Where does the square of a bygone era
begin? Where does it end?
Some cross in an hour, others spend
a life in the crossing:
children in the morning, at evening old men.
How long must they walk on into the sunset
before they can rest?

And how long must they gaze on into the sunset
before they can close their eyes?
When speeding cars turn on their blinding lights.
I see faces: those who once,
on a bright and beautiful morning, crossed the square—
in rearview mirrors, they flash
and disappear.
At dusk, they get in their cars and leave.

A place no one leaves is not a square.
A place where no one falls is not one either.
Those who have left will come again,
those who have fallen will stay forever.
There is a thing called stone: it piles swiftly, stands—
it is nothing like bone, does not take a century to grow
and is not so weak.

Every square has a mind of piled stone,
making the empty-handed people above
feel the weight of survival.
No lighthearted thing, to gaze up and hope with a giant's mind of stone.

石头的重量
减轻了人们肩上的责任、爱情和牺牲。

或许人们会在一个明媚的早晨穿过广场，
张开手臂在四面来风中柔情地拥抱。
但当黑夜降临，双手就变得沉重。
唯一的发光体是脑袋里的石头，
唯一刺向脑袋的利剑悄然坠地。

黑暗和寒冷在上升。
广场周围的高层建筑穿上了瓷和玻璃的时装。
一切变得矮小了。石头的世界
在玻璃反射出来的世界中轻轻浮起，
像是涂在孩子们作业本上的
一个随时会被撕下来揉成一团的阴沉念头。

汽车疾驶而过，把流水的速度
倾注到有着钢铁筋骨的庞大混凝土制度中，
赋予寂静以喇叭的形状。
过去年代的广场从汽车的后视镜消失了。

永远消失了——
一个青春期的、初恋的、布满粉刺的广场。
一个从未在帐单和死亡通知书上出现的广场。
一个露出胸膛、挽起衣袖、扎紧腰带
一个双手使劲搓洗的带补丁的广场。

一个通过年轻的血液流到身体之外
用舌头去舔、用前额去下磕、用旗帜去覆盖
的广场。

The weight of stone
lightens our burden of sacrifice, duty, love.

Perhaps on a bright and beautiful morning people will cross the square
and as the wind rises, tenderly embrace.
But when night draws near, arms grow heavy.
The only light source is the stone in the mind.
The only sword leveled at the mind drops softly to the ground.

Cold and darkness rise.
Office buildings loom on all sides, dressed in the latest styles of tile and glass.
All is made miniature. The world of stone
floats lightly, reflected in the world of glass,
like a scribble in a child's assignment book,
a small dark thought
to be crumpled and thrown away.

Cars hurtle past, fluid speed
pouring through a vast system of steel-tendoned concrete,
silence assuming the shape of a horn.
In rearview mirrors, a square of a bygone era
flashes and is gone.

Gone, forever—
an acne-covered, adolescent square, square of first loves,
a square never figured into ledgers and death counts,
a square of squared shoulders, tightened belts, rolled-up sleeves,
of washboards and hand-me-downs, stitches and patches—

a square that saw youthful blood flow outside of its veins—
a square licked and pounded, knocked by knees and foreheads,
covered in flags—

空想的、消失的、不复存在的广场，
像下了一夜的大雪在早晨停住。
一种纯洁而神秘的融化
在良心和眼睛里交替闪耀，
一部分成为叫做泪水的东西，
一部分在叫做石头的东西里变得坚硬起来。

石头的世界崩溃了。
一个软组织的世界爬到高处。
整个过程就像泉水从吸管离开矿物，
进入蒸馏过的、密封的、有着精美包装的空间。
我乘坐高速电梯在雨天的伞柄里上升。

回到地面时，我抬头看见雨伞一样撑开的
一座圆形餐厅在城市上空旋转。
这是一顶从魔法变出来的帽子，
它的尺寸并不适合
用石头垒起来的巨人的脑袋。

那些曾经托起广场的手臂放了下来。
如今巨人靠一柄短剑来支撑。
它会不会刺破什么呢？比如，曾经有过的
一场在纸上掀起，在墙上张贴的脆弱革命？

从来没有一种力量
能把两个不同的世界长久地粘在一起。
一个反复张贴的脑袋最终将被撕去。
反复粉刷的墙壁，
被露出大腿的混血女郎占据了一半。
另一半是安装假肢、头发再生之类的诱人广告。

一辆婴儿车静静地停在傍晚的广场上，
静静地，和这个快要发疯的世界没有关系。
我猜婴儿车与落日之间的距离

an imagined square, a square that ceased to exist
as a night's snowfall ceases at morning.
A pure and mysterious melting
glistening by turns in consciences and eyes:
one part becoming a thing called tears,
the other hardening into a thing called stone.

The world of stone has crumbled.
Now a cellophane world is rising
like water leaving mineral, creeping up the tube
into a distilled, sealed, charmingly packaged space.
I am riding a high-speed elevator up the handle of an umbrella.

Back on earth, I gaze up at the rooftop restaurant
like an umbrella turning in the sky above the city.
A sorcerer's hat, its dimensions unfit
for a giant's head of piled stone.

The arms that held up the square have let it down.
A giant props himself up with a little sword.
What will he stab? A frail revolution
once incited on paper, plastered on walls?

There is no power
that can keep two worlds pasted together for long.
A paper mind will soon be ripped down.
The gargantuan thigh of a mixed-blood model
bestrides a whitewashed wall
alongside ads for hair restoration, ads for artificial limbs.

A baby carriage stands in the twilit square,
nothing to do with a world nearing madness.
I imagine a distance of about a century

有一百年之遥。
这是近乎无限的尺度，足以测量
穿过广场所经历的一个幽闭时代有多么漫长。

对幽闭的普遍恐惧，
使人们从各自的栖居云集广场，
把一生中的孤独时刻变成热烈的节日。
但在栖居深处，在爱与死的默默注目礼中，
一个空无人迹的影子广场被珍藏着，
像紧闭的忏悔室只属于内心的秘密。

是否穿过广场之前必须穿过内心的黑暗？
现在黑暗中最黑的两个世界合成一体，
坚硬的石头脑袋被劈开，
利剑在黑暗中闪闪发光。

如果我能用劈成两半的神秘黑夜
去解释一个双脚踏在大地上的明媚早晨——
如果我能沿着洒满晨曦的台阶
登上虚无之巅的巨人的肩膀，
不是为了升起，而是为了陨落——
如果黄金镌刻的铭文不是为了被传颂，
而是为了被抹去，被遗忘，被践踏——

正如一个被践踏的广场必将落到践踏者头上，
那些曾在明媚的早晨穿过广场的人
他们的步伐迟早会落到利剑之上，
像必将落下的棺盖落到棺材上那么沉重。
躺在里面的不是我，也不是
行走在剑刃上的人。

separates this child from the sunset.
A century: ruler of almost infinite length, long enough to measure
the span of solitude, the length of a shuttered era.

Fear of solitude
brings the people out of their homes, brings them pouring into the square,
turns life's loneliest hour into a raucous holiday—
but in their darkened homes, where the gazes of love and death meet,
lies a vast empty square, heart's hoard, shadow square
like a shuttered confessional, thing of secrets within.

Before we cross the square, must we first cross the darkness within?
The two halves of darkness have come together.
A mind of hard stone has been cleft in two.
The blade of a sword glitters in the night.

If a strange cleft night can account
for two feet on the ground, for one bright and beautiful morning—
if I am allowed to mount sun-strewn steps
and survey the giddy void from a giant's shoulder
not that I may rise, but that I may fall—
if words engraved on gold plaques are not meant to be sung
but to be rubbed out, to be forgotten, to be trampled—

as a trampled square must one day fall upon the heads of the tramplers,
the footsteps of those who once, on a bright and beautiful morning,
      crossed the square
will fall upon the blade of a sword,
fall heavy, fall as a coffin's lid must fall.
Who lies within? Not me, and not
those who walk on the blade's edge.

我没想到这么多的人会在一个明媚的早晨
穿过广场，避开孤独和永生。
他们是幽闭时代的幸存者。
我没想到他们会在傍晚离去
或倒下。

一个无人倒下的地方不是广场，
一个无人站立的地方也不是。
我曾经是站着的吗？还要站立多久？
毕竟我和那些倒下去的人一样，
从来不是一个永生者。

I had not thought that on bright beautiful mornings, so many
had crossed the square, sundering solitude and eternity.
Survivors of a shuttered era: I had not thought
that at dusk they would leave
or fall.

A place where no one falls is not a square.
A place where no one stands is not one either.
Did I stand? How much longer must I stand?
For I am no different from those who fell—
I am not one to live forever.

II

寂静

站在冬天的橡树下我停止了歌唱
橡树遮蔽的天空像一夜大雪骤然落下
下了一夜的雪在早晨停住
曾经歌唱过的黑马没有归来
黑马的眼睛一片漆黑
黑马眼里的空旷草原积满泪水
岁月在其中黑到了尽头
狂风把黑马吹到天上
狂风把白骨吹进果实
狂风中的橡树就要被连根拔起

Silence

Beneath a winter oak I ceased to sing
The oak-hidden sky came down like snow
A night's snowfall ceased at morning
The black stallion I sang of has not come back
The stallion's eyes were lakes of black
Within which were vast plains flooded with tears
Within which the years swept to black
The wind has blown the stallion into the sky
The wind has blown his bones into fruit
The wind will rip the oak tree from the earth

关于市场经济的虚构笔记

1

从任何变得比它自身更小的窗户
都能看到这个国家，车站后面还是车站。
你的眼睛后面隐藏着一双快速移动的
摄影机的眼睛，喉咙里有一个带旋钮的
通向高压电流的喉咙：录下来的声音，
像剪刀下的卡通动作临时凑在一起，
构成了我们这个时代的视觉特征。
一列蒸汽火车驶离装饰过的现实，一个口号
使庞大的重工业变得轻浮。在口号反面的
广告节目里，政治家走向沿街叫卖的
银行家的封面肖像，手中的望远镜
颠倒过来。他看到的是更为遥远的公众。

2

银行家会不会举手反对省吃俭用的
计划经济的政治美德？花光了挣来的钱，
就花欠下的。如果你把已经花掉的钱
再花一遍，就会变得比存进银行更多，
也更可靠。但是无论你挣多少钱，
数过一遍就变成了假的。一切都在增长
和变化，除了打光子弹的玩具枪，
除了从魔术掏出来的零用钱。
伪装的自传，渗透到公众利益的基础，
从个人积蓄去掉时间，去掉先知先觉的
冰冷常识。如果还不是什么都不需要，幸福
就会越来越少。够吃就行了，没有必要丰收。

Notes Toward a Fiction of the Market Economy

1

Through any window that's become smaller than itself
you'll see this country, land of train stations behind train stations.
Behind your eyes is a pair of hidden tracking camera-eyes,
in your throat a dial-controlled throat running straight
to the power grid, your recorded voice
a series of cartoon motions fluttering from a pair of scissors.
Pieced together, they form the prevailing visual metaphor of our era.
A steam train departs from costumed reality, a slogan
turns heavy industry light as a negligee. On the reverse side
these latest messages show a politician approaching the image
of a banker hawking his wares on magazine covers—
through an inverted telescope he peers at his distant public.

2

Will the bankers raise their voices in dissent
against the penny-saved penny-earned political ideals
of planned economics? Spend what you've made, then spend
what you owe. Spend it again and you'll find you have even more
than if you'd deposited it in the bank. But no matter how much
money you make, count it up and you'll find it's all fake.
It's all growth and change: except for a plastic revolver,
its bullets spent; a nickel pulled from a magic hat.
Masked autobiography has seeped to the root of the public interest,
subtracting time from personal savings, subtracting foresight
and cold common cents. Don't want for nothing and you'll find happiness
steadily shrinking. Give thanks for your meal. Desire no bounty.

3

道德和权力的怀乡病在一句子里
加了括号，不能集中到一个人的嘴上。
你将眼看着身体里长出一个老人，
与感官的玫瑰重合，像什么
就曾经是什么。机器时代的成长
总是在一秒钟的晕眩里嫌一生太漫长。
你知道自己重视的是青春，却选择了一门
到老年才带来荣耀的技艺。要想在年轻时
挥霍老年的巨大财富，必须借助虚无的力量
成为自己身上的死者。大海难以描述的颜色
穿插进来，把你的面孔变成纷乱的小雨，
在加了一道黑边的镜框里突然亮起来。

4

不要那么看重死后的名声，它们
并不真的存在，你能从中腾出手来
去拆一封生前的信。肉体的交谈
没有固定不变的邮政地址，它只对来世
有约束力。只要黑色还在玫瑰中坚持，
爱情就只能通过远处的目光加以注视。
等号后面的目光，它对现存事物的看法
带有回忆录的梦幻性质。要是你转身
转得够快，要是我用第一人称来称呼你：
你可以选择被遗忘还是被记住，下来
还是高踞其上。楼梯已经折叠起来。
你可以取消你的座位，也可以让它停在空中。

3

Your nostalgic notions of authority and morality have become parenthetical,
cut off from the rest of the sentence, prevented from concentrating
on the lips of a single man. You watch as an old man sprouts from your body,
coincident with the rose of the senses, equivalent in his former life
to whatever he is now. Growth in the machine age
will always seem interminable in the daze of an instant.
Though you value your youth, you've chosen a craft
that won't bring glory till your waning years. If you're impatient
to squander the vast coffers of age, you'll find it necessary
to harness the power of the void, become the ghost of your own body.
The indeterminate color of the ocean interposes itself, transforming your face
into flying rain: a flash of light in a black-rimmed mirror.

4

Don't worry about how you'll be remembered by future generations:
free your hand from this myth to open a letter
from your previous life. Conversations in flesh
require no permanent address, and their vows are only binding
in the next. As long as blackness persists in the rose,
love must gaze from the ultimate vantage point.
The eyes behind the equals sign see all extant things
in dreamy memoir-like montage. If you turn quick enough,
if I address you in first person, you can choose
to be forgotten or be remembered, step down
or ascend. The ladder has been folded up.
You can give up your seat, or let it hang in the air.

5

你试图拯救每天的形象：你的家庭生活
将获得一种走了样的国际风格，一种
肥皂剧的轻松调子。凡是曾经出现的
都没有被预言过。美就是对器皿
的空想，先有了一条像空气那么自由的裙子，
然后有一个适合它的腰。你知道色情
比温情更能给女人带来一种理想的美，
其中悲哀的真实成份比假设的、比你
预先想到的还多。干枯的满天星
落到花瓶里，形成腰部紧束的女人，
精神阴暗的另一面。而你满脑袋都是韵脚，
一屁股的欠债像汽水往外冒泡。

6

你谈到旧日女友时引用了新近写下的
一行赞美诗。在头韵和腰韵之间，你假定
肉体之爱是一个叙述中套叙述的
重复过程。重复：措辞的乌托邦。
由此而来的下一个不在此时
此地，其面相带有小地方长大的人
特有的狡猾，加快了来到大城市的步伐。
上班时你混在人群中去见顶头上司，这表明
日出是一种集体印象，与早期教育
所培养的乡土气融成一片。现在没有人
还会惦记故乡，身在何处有什么关系？
飘忽不定的心情，碰巧你是伤感的。

5

Each day is an attempt to salvage your self-image: your
home life assumes a warped international flavor
and mincing soap-opera inflections. Nothing has occurred for which
past predictions haven't failed to account. Beauty is the
idealization of crockery: the space between the curves of a dress
precedes the waist that fits it. Sex
may be better than intimacy as a window into Platonic beauty,
but the truth of the matter is far more pathetic
than your powers of imagination. Pretty bouquet
slips into vase: feminine silhouette bound at the waist.
Flip side of a darkness of spirit. But your head is full of rhyming feet
and arrears are bubbling out your ears.

6

You refer to your old flame with a line borrowed
from a hot new aubade. Between head-rhyme and assonance
bodily affection takes on the appearance
of endless redundant narratives, a neverland of wording. Your next
is never in the here-and-now: her face
has the characteristic slyness of a small-town girl
quickening her steps toward the lights of the big city. At the office
you shoulder among hundreds to see your superior, demonstrating
that the sunrise is a collective image, a blur
of provincialisms instilled by early childhood education.
Who cares where you're from? One place is the same as the next.
Your mind's all over the place: but for the moment, you're homesick.

7

为什么总是那么好，为什么不能
次一些？约会时你到得比上班还晚。
一只脚紧紧踩住加速器，另一只脚
踩在刹车上面。不要向身后回望，
中午的快餐退出视野后会变得广阔起来，
就像暴风雨变成某种性格，在一幅油画中
从推窗可见的田园景色分离出来。
实际上你不可能从旧时代和新生活
去赴同一顿晚餐，幸福
有两种结局，它们都是平庸的。
如果你来晚了就总是来得太晚，
如果来得早了一点，约会就将取消。

8

起初你要什么，主人就在杯子里
给你斟满什么。现在杯子里是什么
你就得喝什么。下一个轮到你去白净的
洗手间，把想要呕吐的全部呕吐出来。
这顿午餐在本质上是黑夜。要是它的真实性
再减少一些，看上去就会像催眠似地
让人着迷。从中裂开的幽暗酒吧，
对于一把餐刀是开心果，但如果使用的
是筷子，仅有的饥饿将倾向于放弃肉体。
食谱里的花朵，是否能够借助光线的变化
显示被风刮过，或是被刀子扎过的
不同黑暗？尽管触及黑暗的花梗已经折断。

7

Why does it always have to be so good? Why can't it be
just average once in a while? You arrive at your date
later than you do for work. One foot on the accelerator,
other on the brake. Don't look back: your fast-food lunch
will expand into infinity upon retreating from view
like a storm distilled out of a pastoral sky
and onto a canvas, assuming personal qualities.
After all, past and present can't deliver you
to the same dinner table. Happiness
has two possible endings, both of them humdrum.
Once late, twice late, always too late:
but don't be early or she'll cancel the date.

8

Whoever's picking up the tab will pour you a glass
of whatever you want, but then all you've got
is whatever was just poured in your glass. Then it's your turn
to disgorge into the gleaming white bathroom sink
whatever it was you wanted to disgorge. The midday repast
has been displaced to midnight. If it got any less real
it would lull you into a hypnosis-like dream-state,
splitting open to reveal the nightclub's shadowy interior,
like a nut to a steak knife: but if you used chopsticks,
your only hunger might forsake the flesh. Can the cookbook's flowers
adequately reflect, in the changing light, the wind-tossed knife-slashed
varieties of darkness? Though their roots in night have snapped.

9

起伏的蛇腰穿过两端，其长度
可以任意延长，只要事物的短暂性
还在起作用。犯人在被抓住之后
才有面孔，然而本来就不那么肯定的证据
否定不了什么，也不可能被否定。
辩护词是从另一桩案子摘抄下来的，
其要点写进了教科书。从前的进修生
摇身变成法官，他的外省口音
听上去带有大蒜发芽的味道，使两个
彼此接近的事实变得必须单独面对。
法律从嗓子沙哑的遗产纠纷中取消了
抑扬格，把它转变成一道空想的象棋难题。

10

这个国家只有一个窗口出售车票。火车
就要进站了。你想象自己在空中居住，
有一个偶然想到的地址，和一个
天文数字构成的电话号码。当你散步
经过保险公司，终生积蓄象搓过的耳朵
来到烈酒表面，也许它们最终将在羞涩
和屈辱的相互忘却之间冻得通红。硬币
或纸币：你不可能成为甜蜜生活的骨头。
眼睛充满安静的泪水，与怒火保持恰当的
比例。河流总是在远方。大地上的列车
按照正确的时间法则行驶，不带抒情成分。
你知道自己不是新一代人。"忘记我在这里。"

9

A snake has a waist of potentially infinite length,
as long as the brevity of the current turn
continues to be felt. A felon has no face
until he's caught, but the undeniable evidence
denies nothing at all, the burden of proof has been lifted
from another case, the sentence copied word-for-word
from a textbook, and the voice of justice
has a backcountry drawl and a two-year degree
from a community college where they taught him to reason
that two similar things are irreconcilable opposites.
Law repeals rhyme from hoarse inheritance disputes,
reducing emotions to moves on a chessboard.

10

This country has only one ticket window. The train
will be arriving momentarily. You imagine yourself living in the sky
with a random address and an astronomical phone number.
When you walk past the insurance company your life savings come
quick as a rub at the ears to the surface of a shot of pure
alcohol: perhaps between the twin amnesias of sheepishness and shame
they'll go bright red. Credit or debit: neither can give bones
to your honeyed fantasies. Your eyes are placid pools of tears mixed
in exact proportion with the fires of rage, the river remains
on the horizon, and all the trains on the earth continue
to arrive and depart according to heartless timetables.
You know you're an old-timer. "Forget that I'm here."

去雅典的鞋子

这地方已经呆够了。
总得去一趟雅典——
多年来，你赤脚在田野里行走。
梦中人留下一双去雅典的鞋子，
你却在纽约把它脱下。

在纽约街头你开鞋店，
贩卖家乡人懒散的手工活路，
贩卖他们从动物换来的脚印，
从春天树木砍下来的双腿——
这一切对文明是有吸引力的。

但是尤利西斯的鞋子
未必适合你梦想中的美国，
也未必适合观光时代的雅典之旅。
那样的鞋子穿在脚上
未必会使文明人走向荷马。

他们不会用砍伐的树木行走，
也不会花钱去买死人的鞋子，
即使花掉的是死人的金钱。
一双气味扰人的鞋要走出多远
才能长出适合它的双脚？

关掉你的鞋店。请想象
巨兽穿上彬彬有礼的鞋
去赴中产阶级的体面晚餐。
请想象一只孤零零的芭蕾舞脚尖
在巨兽的不眠夜踮起。

Athens Shoes

Enough of this place: you're off to Athens.
Too many years spent barefoot in the fields.
In a dream, a woman gave you a pair of sandals
to walk to Athens
but New York was where you took them off.

On a Manhattan street corner you opened a cobbler's stand
and plied your ancestors' lazy trade,
peddling the footprints they bought from animals,
your own legs severed from a tree in spring:
objects of interest to civilization.

But the shoes of Ulysses do not fit
the America you dream, and the Sightseeing Age
is not the time for a trip to Athens.
Your sandals won't make modern feet
walk down the road to Homer.

These people don't want to walk on your wooden legs,
and they wouldn't buy dead people's shoes, even if
they held immortal currency.
How far must those sweet-scented sandals walk
before they grow their pair of feet?

Close down your stand. Imagine, if you will,
a monstrous beast in respectable shoes
on his way to a bourgeois dinner party.
Imagine the toe of a ballerina
en pointe in his sleepless nights.

请想象一个人失去双腿之后
仍然在奔跑。雅典远在千里之外。
哦孤独的长跑者：多年来
他的假肢有力地敲打大地，
他的鞋子在深渊飞翔——

你未必希望那是雅典之旅的鞋子。

Imagine: a man who has lost both legs
still running, running. And Athens—oceans away.
Pity the lone runner, his artificial legs
flogging the ground for years without end
while a pair of sandals wing through the abyss—

don't let those be your Athens shoes.

风筝火鸟

飞起来，飞起来该多好，
但飞起来的并非都是鸟儿。

我对香槟酒到处都在相碰感到厌倦了。
这是春天，人人都在呕吐。

是呕吐出来的楼梯在飞翔，
是一座摩天楼从胃里呕吐出来。

生活的帐单随四月的风刮了过去。
然后剃刀接着刮，五月接着刮。

是的，自由人的身体是词语做的，
可以随手扔进废纸篓，

也可以和天使的身体对折起来，
获得天上的永久地址。

鸟儿从邮差手里递了过来，
按照风的原样保持在吹拂中。

无论这是朝向剪刀飞翔的鸟儿，
印刷的、沿街张贴的鸟儿；

还是铁丝缠身的竹子的鸟儿，
被处以火刑的纸的鸟儿——

你首先是灰烬
然后仍旧是灰烬。

The Burning Kite

What a thing it would be, if we all could fly.
But to rise on air does not make you a bird.

I'm sick of the hiss of champagne bubbles.
It's spring, and everyone's got something to puke.

The things we puke: flights of stairs,
a skyscraper soaring from the gut,

the bills blow by on the April breeze
followed by flurries of razor blades in May.

It's true, a free life is made of words.
You can crumple it, toss it in the trash,

or fold it between the bodies of angels, attaining
a permanent address in the sky.

The postman hands you your flight of birds
persisting in the original shape of wind.

Whether they're winging toward the scissors' V
or printed and plastered on every wall

or bound and trussed, bamboo frames wound with wire
or sentenced to death by fire

you are, first
and always, ash.

一根断线，两端都连着狂风。
救火车在大地上急驰。

但这壮烈的大火是天上的事情。
手里的杯子高高抛起。

没有人知道，飞翔在一人独醒的天空，
那种迷醉，那种玉石俱焚的迷醉。

Broken wire, a hurricane at each end.
Fire trucks scream across the earth.

But this blaze is a thing of the air.
Raise your glass higher, toss it up and away.

Few know this kind of dizzy glee:
an empty sky, a pair of burning wings.

我们的睡眠，我们的饥饿

1

飨宴带着风格的垂涎升起。
侍者们在天空中站立了一夜，
没有梯子可以下来。
蜡烛的微弱光亮独自攀登。
那样一种高度显然不适合你，
当你试着从更高的饥饿去看待幸福。
幸福只是低低吹来的晨风，
弯腰才能碰到。

2

阴影比飨宴更低地低下来
等待豹子出现。豹子的饥饿
是一种精神上的处境，
拥有家族编年史的广阔篇幅，
但不保留咀嚼的锯齿形痕迹，
没有消化，没有排泄，
表达了对食物的敬意
以及对精神洁癖的向往。

Our Hunger, Our Sleep

1

The banquet rises, dripping the slaver of style.
The servants stand in the sky all night,
no steps to let them down.
The flame of a candle feebly aspires.
You are not suited to such heights,
to gaze down at happiness from a higher hunger.
Happiness is a low-blowing morning breeze:
to reach it, you must stoop.

2

Down, down, far below the banquet, shadows
await the coming of the leopard. His hunger
is a condition of the spirit,
voluminous as bloodlines, millennial annals,
but bearing not a single jagged tooth-mark,
free of digestion and excretion,
an expression of reverence for food
and yearning for austerity.

3

蝙蝠的出现不需要天空。
蝙蝠紧贴蝙蝠飞来——
这混血的、经过伪装的飞行，
面目是从老鼠变来的，
但是肉体的其他部分
与我们白日所见的鸟类一致。
蝙蝠把阳光涂抹在底片上，加深
我们对睡眠和黑夜的依赖。

4

人在睡眠中发明了一些飞鸟，
一些好听的叫声，洁白的
松弛的羽毛。但它们只是
关于飞行的官方说法。
而蝙蝠没有白天的住处，
它的天空是一个地下天空，
能见度低于一只蜡烛。
吹灭目光，让灰烬安静地升起。

3

The bat's arrival does not require sky.
Bat tight on bat they spiral forth—
a camouflaged and mongrel flight,
a face transfigured from the rat's,
though the rest of his body bears a similarity
to the birds we see by day.
The bat smears daylight across a negative plate, deepening
our dependence on sleep, our addiction to darkness.

4

We in our sleep have invented birds,
invented song, invented pure
white feathers. But birds
are just the party line on flight:
the bat has no residence in light, his sky
is an underground sky, lower than the visibility
provided by a guttering candle.
Extinguish sight: ash rises in peaceful spirals.

5

睡眠遮蔽睡眠有如蝙蝠收回翅膀。
你在某处呆着，起身离去的
是千里之外敲门的豹子，
它的饥饿是一座监狱的饥饿，
自由的门朝向武器敞开。
蝙蝠的天空在早晨消失了，
给大地留下深深刻画的失眠症，
擦亮了黑暗深处的钥匙。

6

你睡去时听到了神秘的敲门声。
是死者在敲门：他们想干什么呢？
在两种真相之间没有门可以推开。
于是你脱下鞋子与豹子交换足迹，
摘下眼镜给近视的蝙蝠戴，
并且拿出伤感的金钱让死者花。
你醒来时发现身上的锁链
像豹子的优美条纹长进肉里。

5

Sleep covers sleep as a bat folds back his wings.
While you linger, a thousand miles off
the leopard who was knocking at the door
turns and leaves. His hunger is a prison wall,
and the only door opens onto gunfire.
When morning comes the bat's sky disappears,
leaving the print of insomnia on the earth,
revealing a key glinting in the dark.

6

You hear a knocking in your sleep.
The dead are knocking. What do they want?
A door cannot connect realities.
So you trade footprints with the leopard,
bequeath your glasses to the myopic bat,
and to the dead offer up the currency of sentiment.
You wake to find your chains grown
into your skin like the leopard's lovely stripes.

7

孑然一身站在大地上的人,
被天空中躺下的人重重压着。
躺下来的身体多少有些相似,
差异性如其他动物的皮毛
在睡眠中闪耀。一条羊毛毯子
从星空滑落下来,覆盖你的蝴蝶梦,
但梦中并没一个庄子让你阅读。
你未必希望读的是孔夫子。

8

多年来,你在等一顿天上的晚餐。
那些迟来的人从老式楼梯
走了上来,但没有椅子可以坐下。
对我们是合在一起的食物,
对豹子则是单独的。这是高贵的飨宴:
你点菜的时候用豹子的艰深语言。
如此博学的饥饿:你几乎
感觉不到饥饿,除非给它一点兽性。

7

A man stands alone on the face of the earth,
pressed by the multiplied weight of those who lie
in the sky above, reiterated forms like hairs
glinting on the bodies of other animals
as they sleep. A fur blanket slips from space
and covers up your butterfly dreams.
But in this dream, there is no Zhuangzi.
And Confucius might not be what you want to read.

8

All these years you've waited for your banquet in the sky.
Now latecomers mount the antique stairs to find
not a seat remains. You stand all night.
We eat in the plural, but the leopard dines
in the singular. What a lofty affair:
you order your dish in the leopard's abstruse tongue.
O hunger: such a recondite thing, it cannot be felt
unless mixed with a bit of beastliness.

9

食物简洁地升起。谁也不知道
你在晚餐中放了多少盐，
这是生活本身的秘密。
为什么人会在夜里感到口渴？
喝光了大地的水，就喝天上的。
下了一夜的雨需要嗓子和眼睛
来保存，需要一个水龙头来拧紧，
温柔地、细而小地流向羞耻心。

10

水聚集在一起泼都泼不掉。
大海溢出但我们的仓库和杯子
依然是空的。瞧这片大海，
它哪里在乎盛水的身子是含金的
还是朽木的。不要指望无边的幸福
能够为你保存小一些的幸福，
像龋齿中的黑色填充物那么小，
碰到了年深日久的痛楚。

9

Food rises by virtue of its purity. Who knows
how much salt you added to your meal?
This is life's riddle: why we wake thirsty in the night.
You've drunk up the earth's water,
now drink the sky's. A night of rain
needs a throat and a pair of eyes
to hold it, needs a tap screwed tight:
drip, water, drip. Gently irrigate our shame.

10

Water, once collected, will not pour.
The ocean overflows, and yet
our cups and storehouses remain empty.
Look at that ocean—it doesn't give a damn
if the vessels that hold its water are gold
or rot. A horizonless happiness can't contain
your smaller happiness, a tiny daub of black
in a tooth holding back the tiny ache of years.

11

牙痛的豹子：随它怎样去捕食吧，
它那辽阔的胃如掌声传开。
但这一切纯属我们头脑里的产物，
采取暴力的高级形式朝心灵移动，
仿佛饥饿是一门古老的技艺，
它的容貌是不起变化的
时间的容貌：食物是它的镜子。
而我们则依赖我们的衰老活到今天。

12

蝙蝠的夜晚是被颠倒的白昼。
在那样一种黑暗中看得很远，
回到光芒就会悲哀地瞎掉。
光芒在蝙蝠身上已经瞎了，
它睁开人类的眼睛
看待自己，视力隐入另一类自然。
作为一只鸟儿的老鼠在飞翔，
但老鼠天性中的鸟儿却失去了天空。

11

Toothaching leopard: let him go ahead and prey.
Let his vast gut disseminate
like applause. But all this is just
a thing of our minds, this co-opting the rarefied
order of violence to approach the spirit,
as if Hunger were an ancient art, its face
the unchanging face of Time, and Food its mirror.
And we've relied on Age to live until today.

12

The bat's night is the inverted image of day.
After seeing so far in that kind of darkness,
the bat returns to light heart-rent,
eye-lorn. Light, when it shines on a bat,
is blind: it has borrowed the eyes of humanity
to regard itself, vision assuming
its cryptic form. The rat-that-is-bird
wings on, but the bird has lost its sky.

13

如果去赴晚餐，一定是在天上。
双手按下电钮让餐桌静静地升起，
但我们的饥饿真有那么高吗？
当豹子像烈酒一样忍受着丰收
和分配，当蝙蝠在墙上变成白色。
昨夜的雨是你多年前晒过的阳光。
太阳的初次销魂是一只蜡烛，
照耀没人在的卧室和厨房。

13

When you sit down to dinner, you eat in the sky.
The table rises, as if by an invisible mechanism.
Is our hunger really so high?
When the leopard, like spirit, endures dilution
and gain; when the bat's body on the wall turns white.
Last night's rain was last year's light.
The sun's apotheosis is the glimmer of a candle
illuminating empty bedrooms, empty kitchens.

谁去谁留

黄昏，那小男孩躲在一株植物里
偷听昆虫的内脏。他实际听到的
是昆虫以外的世界：比如，机器的内脏。
落日在男孩脚下滚动有如卡车轮子，
男孩的父亲是卡车司机，
卡车卸空了
       停在旷野上。
父亲走到车外，被落日的一声不吭的美惊呆了。
他挂掉响个不停的行动电话，
对男孩说：天边滚动的万事万物都有嘴唇，
但它们只对物自身说话，
只在这些话上建立耳朵和词。
    男孩为否定物的耳朵而偷听了内心的耳朵。
他实际上不在听，
却意外听到了一种完全不同的听法——
那男孩发明了自己身上的聋，
他成了飞翔的、幻想的聋子。
会不会在凡人的落日后面
另有一个众声喧哗的神迹世界？
会不会另有一个人在听，另有一个落日
在沉落？
    哦踉跄的天空
大地因没人接听的电话而异常安静。
机器和昆虫彼此没听见心跳，
植物也已连根拔起。
那小男孩的聋变成了梦境，秩序，乡音。

Who Is Gone, and Who Remains

Dusk: the boy hides in a tree-root,
eavesdropping on the innards of insects.
What he hears is not the world of insects
but the world outside: for example, innards of machines.
The setting sun turns beneath his feet like the wheel of a truck,
the boy's father drives a truck
the truck is empty
                              parked in an empty field.
The father gets out, and the soundless beauty of the sunset strikes him dumb.
He turns off his crying cell phone, says to the boy:
all things turning at the edge of the sky
have lips, have tongues. But they speak only amongst themselves,
erecting their ears upon this speech.
          The boy, refusing to believe in the ears of things, listens to the ears
                              of his heart.
In truth, he is not listening at all,
but, by not listening, he overhears
a different kind of hearing—
he invents his own deafness, and soars,
rising on mute updrafts of imagination.
Behind our everyday sunset, could there be
a miracle-world alive with voices?
Could there be another boy listening, another sun
sinking in the west?
                    Staggering sky—
The world has fallen silent: a telephone rings on, unanswered.
Machines and insects cannot hear each other's heartbeats,
and the root has been ripped from the soil.
The boy's deafness becomes dream-vision, protocol, brogue.

卡车开不动了
                              父亲在埋头修理。
而母亲怀抱落日睡了一会，只是一会，
不知天之将黑，不知老之将至。

The truck is broken

                         his father buries his head under the hood
and his mother sleeps, sunset cradled in her arms, unaware
of the coming of night, the coming of age.

毕加索画牛

接下来的两个星期毕加索在画牛。
那牛身上似乎有一种越画得多
也就越少的古怪现象。
"少"艺术家问，"能变成多吗？"
"一点不错，"毕加索回答说。
批评家等着看画家的多。

但那牛每天看上去都更加稀少。
先是蹄子不见了，跟着牛角没了，
然后牛皮像视网膜一样脱落，
露出空白之间的一些接榫。
"少，要少到什么地步才会多起来？"
"那要看你给多起什么名字。"

批评家感到迷惑。
"是不是你在牛身上拷打一种品质，
让地中海的风把肉体刮得零零落落？"
"不单是风在刮，瞧对面街角
那间肉铺子，花枝招展的女士们，
每天都从那儿割走几磅牛肉。"

"从牛身上，还是从你的画布上割？"
"那得看你用什么刀子。"
"是否美学和生活的伦理学在较量？"
"挨了那么多刀，哪来的力气。"
"有什么东西被剩下了？"
"不，精神从不剩下。赞美浪费吧。"

Picasso Paints a Bull

Over the course of the next two weeks Picasso will paint a bull.
A bull whose body seems possessed by a strange reality:
the more Picasso paints, the less there is.
"Can less"—the artist asks—"become more?"
"Right on," Picasso replies.
The critic waits to see the painter's more.

But Picasso's bull just keeps getting scarcer.
The hooves are first to go—then the horns,
then the skin itself drops off like a retina,
revealing the joints between empty spaces.
"How less does it have to get before it becomes more?"
"That depends on the name you give to more."

The critic is confused. "Would you say that in this work
you are committing moral violence on the bovine body,
shearing off every scrap of flesh with your Mediterranean wind?"
"Don't blame the wind—look at that butcher shop
across the way. Every day I watch lovely young ladies
walk home with a few dozen pounds of his meat."

"Whose meat? The meat of the bull on your canvas?"
"Now that depends on which knife you use."
"Is this a contest between the ethics of aesthetics and the ethics of life?"
"All cut up, how'd he have energy for that?"
"And what's left over? Anything?"
"No, no spirit remains. Praise waste."

"你的牛对世界是一道减法吗？"
"为什么不是加法？我想那肉店老板
正在演算金钱。"第二天老板的妻子
带着毕生积蓄来买毕加索画的牛。
但她看到的只是几根简单的线条。
"牛在哪儿呢？"她感到受了冒犯。

"Is your bull an act of subtraction upon the world?"
"Why not addition? I imagine that butcher is
counting his cash right now." Sure enough, the next day,
the butcher's wife comes with her life savings to buy Picasso's bull.
But all she sees are a couple lines.
"Where's the bull?" she asks, indignant.

III

手枪

手枪可以拆开
拆作两件不相关的东西
一件是手，一件是枪
枪变长可以成为一个党
手涂黑可以成为另一个党

而东西本身可以再拆
直到成为相反的向度
世界在无穷的拆字法中分离

人用一只眼睛寻求爱情
另一只眼睛压进枪膛
子弹眉来眼去
鼻子对准敌人的客厅
政治向左倾斜
一个人朝东方开枪
另一个人在西方倒下

黑手党戴上白手套
长枪党改用短枪
永远的维纳斯站在石头里
她的手拒绝了人类
从她的胸脯拉出两只抽屉
里面有两粒子弹，一枝枪
要扣响时成为玩具
谋杀，一次哑火

Handgun (II)

after Ouyang Jianghe

a handgun can be disassembled
into unrelated things:
a hand, a gun
a hand plus its opposite equals a weapon
a gun plus its opposite equals itself

things taken apart
can't be put back together
a hand plus a gun is a change in the weather
high against low
east against west
reality divides
along infinite fronts

guns shoot without hands
hands kill without guns
in the east, a finger presses a button
in the west, a man falls

in bedrooms and offices
hands grip objects they've named
while steel forgets its shape
and distant caves rattle
with notions of rain

母亲，厨房

在万古与一瞬之间，出现了开合与渺茫。
在开合深处，出现了一道门缝。
门后面，是被推开的厨房。

菜刀起落处，云卷云舒。
光速般合拢的生死
被切成星球的两半，慢的两半。

萝卜也切成了两半。
在厨房，母亲切了悠悠一生，
一盘凉拌三丝，切得千山万水，
一条鱼，切成逶迤游刃的样子，
端上餐桌还不肯离开池塘。

暑天的豆腐，被切出了雪意，
而土豆听命于洋葱般的刀法
和顿挫，一种如花吐瓣的剥落，
一种时间内部的物我两空。
去留之间，刀起刀落。

但母亲手上并没有拿刀。

天使们递到母亲手上的
不是刀，是几片落叶。
深海的秋刀鱼越过刀锋
朝星空游去。如今厨房在天上，
整个菜市场被塞进冰箱，
而母亲，已无力打开冷时间。

Mother, Kitchen

Where the immemorial and the instant meet, opening and distance appear.
Through the opening: a door, crack of light.
Behind the door, a kitchen.

Where the knife rises and falls, clouds gather, disperse.
A lightspeed joining of life and death, cut
in two: halves of a sun, of slowness.

Halves of a turnip.
A mother in the kitchen, a lifetime of cuts.
A cabbage cut into mountains and rivers,
a fish, cut along its leaping curves,
laid on the table
still yearning for the pond.

Summer's tofu
cut into premonitions of snow.
A potato listens to the onion-counterpoint
of the knife, dropping petals at its strokes:
self and thing, halves of nothing
at the center of time.
Where gone and here meet, the knife rises, falls.

But this mother is not holding a knife.

What she has been given is not a knife
but a few fallen leaves.
The fish leaps over the blade from the sea
to the stars. The table is in the sky now,
the market has been crammed into the refrigerator,
and she cannot open cold time.

给"H": 在VERMONT过53岁生日

1

等待一生的八月，九月之后才到来。
先秦的月亮，在弗尔蒙特升起。
一个退思，在光的星期五移动。
庄子朝我走来，
以离我而去的脚步。
云移的脚步，花开的脚步，邮政系统的脚步。

2

一封春秋来信，
至今没有投递到我的手上。
邮差在天空中飞来飞去。
地球那边，你在读信。
还没写的信，你已经读到了我。
一封我拆开了两次的信，你一次也没寄出。
一些预先开花的，将要破土的，空的声音。

For "H"

—on turning 53 in Vermont

1

A long-awaited August, arriving in September.
An ancient moon, rising in Vermont.
Memories, moving in the light from Friday.
Zhuangzi approaches
with receding footsteps.
Footsteps of cloud patterns, unfolding petals, postal systems.

2

A letter written in an ancient autumn
has not yet found its way into my hand.
The postman is winging through the blue.
On the other side of the earth, you're reading a letter I've yet to write.
You've yet to send
a letter I've already opened twice.
Preflowered, unbroken, empty voices.

3

电话里传来落花般的女高音。
那是你么，把花开到灯里去的声音？
打给HELLO的电话，接听的是一个喂。
喂的外面，中餐馆人声鼎沸，
一群食客饿坏了，但厨师是画师，
他将牛排画成水墨，端给看客吃。
一头观念的牛比真的更值钱吗？
刚断奶的单身母亲，把马克思
像奶嘴一样塞进婴儿嘴里，
阻止牛奶发出无产者的尖叫声。
而银行家用头脑里的提款机
一夜之间，提空了内心。

4

在金钱的声音被挂断之后，
诗的声音是什么？
一只神秘的手按下免提键。
现在，手机是广播，
全世界都在听这个声音。
李尔王能听到他的莎士比亚吗？
萨福的月亮，能从李白的月亮
听到庄子化蝶的风吹雪吗？
我能听到另一个我吗？
但在你的铃声响起之前，
只有无止境的，宇宙洪荒般的寂静。

3

I pick up your call. I hear your lilting voice.
A sound to open blossoms in lamps, that voice.
I say hello, you answer *wei?*
In the background, the din of a Chinese banquet hall.
The guests are starving, but the chef is an artist
who paints ribeyes in ink, serves them on a scroll.
Is the concept of *cow* worth more than the meat?
A weaning mother crams the teat of Marx
between her infant's lips, suppressing the milk's
proletarian yelps, while a banker
at the ATM machine inside his own head
presses the button to empty his heart.

4

When we've hung up on the voice of money,
will we hear poetry's voice?
An invisible finger presses a button:
the world is on speakerphone.
Will King Lear hear Shakespeare calling?
Will Li Bai hear, in Sappho's moon,
the wind-blown snow of a butterfly's dream?
Will I hear my other me?
In the minutes before my cell phone rings—
astral, primordial silence.

5

可以用生日蜡烛点燃一个无我。
可以把明信片上的纸火焰
从古中国快递到黄昏的弗尔蒙特。
可以借蝴蝶夜的灰尘，轻盈一吹。
可以吹灭我的心。
心那么易碎，那么澎湃，可以和宇宙
构成一个尖锐，
一个小，无限大的极小。
一个53年的十亿光年。

6

如果只有一个过去，我就是这个过去。
如果我的现在有五百个过去，
那么一个现在我都没有。
你呢，你有第二个现在吗？
或许，你在你不在的地方，而我不是
我是的人。我有两个旧我，其中一个
刚刚新生：一个53岁的
吾丧我。

5

Strike a match, light an anti-me.
Send the paper flames of your postcards express
from ancient China to twilit Vermont.
Blow lightly, light as wings turned to dust.
Blow out my heart.
Brittle heart, billowing heart, which together with the universe
composes a point:
a smallness of infinite size,
the million light years of fifty-three years.

6

If I have only one past, I am that past.
But if I have five hundred pasts
then I don't have a single present.
Do you have another present?
Perhaps you are not where you are, and I am not
who I am. I have two past selves, one of them
newborn: a 53-year old
no one at all.

7

一条鱼躺在晚餐的盘子里，
被刀切过，被炉火烤过。
这是一个发生。
同一条鱼从河里游到电脑界面，
以超现实的目光看着我。
这也是一个发生。
人可以演奏鱼的音乐么，
从物种的同一性演奏出一个悖反？
比如，将盘子里的鱼演奏成厨师，
将水中鱼演奏成一个哲学家。
但是庄子在演奏更神秘的生命，
一条烤熟的鱼，在天空中游动起来。

8

宇宙是科学老人的玩具。
孩子们站在地球仪上要糖吃。
一个梦的工程师，转动这只地球仪，
并将乌托邦转手给天边外的鹤。
一只鹤，即使是纸的，也在天空中飞，
即使看起来像工程吊臂，也在舞蹈，
用足尖踮起心之鹤形。
庄子骋怀纵目，以鹤作为引导。
而你将鹤止步放进万马齐奔，
并以水仙般的鹤立，支起一个梦工地。

7

A fish lies on a dinner plate,
cut by knife, cooked by flame.
This can happen.
The same fish swims up out of the river and onto my keyboard,
where it studies me with surreal eyes—
this can also happen.
Can a human play the music of the fish,
play an inversion against the parallel motion of species?
Play a chef out of the fish on the plate,
a philosopher out of the fish in the river?
But Zhuangzi is playing at something far stranger:
a cooked fish, swimming to life in the sky.

8

The universe is an elderly scientist's toy.
A kid stands on the globe, demanding a lollipop.
An engineer spins the world in his hand,
then turns, hands paradise to a crane beyond the sky.
A crane, even of paper, remains in flight—
and despite its steel cousin, continues
to dance, stand on tiptoe: crane-stance of the heart.
Zhuangzi follows the crane's example.
He stands tall, looks far, unbridles his spirit.
And you give motionless poise to the thunder of horses,
balance the foundation of a dream atop the stem of a narcissus.

9

人置身于桃花源，桃花就凋落了。
拥有太多末日和诞生，时间就消失了。
痛，也消失了。一只电钻
在大地的龋齿上钻洞。
神经末梢的听觉之痛，将牙科诊所
安放在地球的寂静深处。
每天，钻头，在痛的深处加深几毫米。
要是再深一些，人心，就能深及地心，
喷泉般，喷涌出一个璀璨的地下天空，
一株天体物理的火树银花。

10

庄子的胡须在秋风中飘动。
这只是史蒂文斯头脑里的一个幻象。
我递过一个电动剃须刀。
现在，我们三个人的三个下巴
有了同一颗电池的心：时间转动，
反时间也在转动。庄子的月亮
被退回先秦。我每天使用剃须刀。
古代是我的现代，而我只是一个仿古。

9

When we set foot in paradise, peach blossoms wither.
Time fades, worn by beginnings and endings.
Pain fades. A jackhammer
bores into the teeth of the earth.
The ache of human ears: an endodontist's chair
placed in the hushed nave of the planet.
Every day, we bore a few inches deeper.
Any deeper, and our hearts would touch.
And an underground sky would gush forth, fountain-like,
pyrotechnic flowers unfolding in space.

10

The beard of Zhuangzi, moving in the wind—
this is just a picture in the mind of Stevens.
I offer them both an electric razor.
Now, our three chins
have the same small battery-powered heart:
time turns, anti-time turns.
An ancient moon, returned to China unanswered—
every day, I use my razor.
The past is my present.
I'm a reproduction.

驻足于隔世的月光，我等待你的足音，
等待一个刹那溢出终极性。
我真的到过弗尔蒙特吗？
一米之遥，人已在千里外的异乡。
夜空中，我看不见一棵松树，
但松果漫天掉落。生命
也这样掉落，像一只中国古瓮。
空，落地，我俯身拾起无限多的空。
每一片具体的碎片里，都有一个抽象。
词和肉体，已逝和重现，拼凑
并粘连起来，形成一个透彻。
世界回复最初的脆弱
和圆满，今夜深梦无痕。
但古瓮将又一次摔落。

11

Beneath the moon of a different world
I pause, listening for your footsteps, waiting
for the moment from which eternity will spill.
Am I really in Vermont?
A distance of an inch puts you in another country.
I can't see the pine trees in the dark,
but pine cones are falling everywhere.
Life is falling, like a porcelain urn.
Empty, falling.
I stoop, gather the shards of its emptiness.
Every shard, both instance and idea,
word and flesh, past and future.
Pieced together, they make a finality.
And the world is once again fragile and full,
the night unmarred.
Though this is not the last time the urn will fall.

Appendix: "Handgun"

"Handgun" is a poem for which wordplay is so central that it defies any conventional kind of translation. But as it's one of Ouyang's most influential poems, I feel compelled to represent it somehow in this anthology.

To do this I've written two versions. The first mimics more closely the verbal choreography of the poem, splitting words and recapitulating ideas at the same moments as the original, though by necessity the words and ideas are slightly different. But through its loyalty to the poem's movements on the micro-level, it sacrifices the larger philosophical resonance. The second version is meant as a gesture towards this lost resonance, though to pursue a similar argument in English one must essentially write a different poem. My hope is that by superimposing these two silhouettes the reader might imagine the original in the round.

Those curious to see what Ouyang is actually doing can consult the following annotated "literal" version.

Handgun

a handgun can be taken apart
into two unrelated things
a hand and a gun
a gun lengthened becomes a Party
> (党 *dang* = any faction or political party)

a hand painted black becomes another Party

and things themselves can be further disassembled
> (东西 *dongxi* = thing, object; the
> characters 东 *dong* and 西 *xi* mean east
> and west, respectively)

into pairs of opposing dimensions
the world divides in infinite character-parsings

> (拆字法 *chaizifa* = the practice of parsing
> Chinese words into separate characters
> or characters into separate components,
> traditionally for the purposes of fortune-
> telling)

with one eye we look for love
the other we ram down the barrel
the bullets ogle
our noses aim at enemies' parlors
politics tilt leftward
a man shoots into the east
in the west, a man falls

the Mafia put on white gloves

> (黑手党 *heishoudang*, lit. "Black Hand
> Party," is the generic Chinese word for
> gangsters)

the Falangists switch to pistols

> (长枪党 *changqiangdang*, lit. "Long Gun
> Party," is the Chinese name for the
> Falangists of Spain or Lebanon. 长枪
> *changqiang* "long gun" originally meant
> spear, hence phalanx, hence Falangists.)
> (短枪 *duanqiang*, lit. "short gun," means
> handgun or pistol)

eternal Venus stands in stone
her hands rejecting humanity
from her chest she pulls a pair of drawers
inside, two bullets and a gun
pull the trigger and it becomes a toy
murder, hang fire

Acknowledgments

Grateful acknowledgment is made to the editors of *Asymptote, Chutzpah!* (天南), *Kenyon Review Online, Poetry,* and *Zoland Poetry,* where some of these poems originally appeared.

In addition, my heartfelt thanks go out to all those who offered me their advice, guidance, support, and encouragement during my long search for an English voice for Ouyang: Lydia Liu, Christopher Mattison, Sandy McClatchy, Gary Clark, Sierra Nelson, Cole Swensen, Eliot Weinberger, Jenny Blair, Charlie Gershman, Nate Klug, Perry Link, Tian Xi, Anne Chang, Wang Hongjian, Robert Polito, Bakhyt Kenjeev, Nikki Greenwood, and many others. And most of all I am indebted to Ouyang himself for welcoming me into his home, cheerfully putting up with my endless questions, and giving so much of his own time at every step of the process.

Thanks also to the Vermont Studio Center and the Jintian Literary Foundation, whose support made my collaboration with Ouyang possible.

—*Austin Woerner*

JINTIAN SERIES OF CONTEMPORARY LITERATURE

In Print

Flash Cards
Yu Jian
Translated by Wang Ping & Ron Padgett

The Changing Room
Zhai Yongming
Translated by Andrea Lingenfelter

Forthcoming

A Phone Call from Dalian
Han Dong
Edited and Translated by Nicky Harman,
with contributions from Maghiel van Crevel,
Michael Day, Tao Naikan, Tony Prince, and Yu Yan Chen
Introduction by Maghiel van Crevel

Wind Says
Bai Hua
Translated by Fiona Sze Lorraine